CM00924034

How Snow Falls

HOW

SNOW

FALLS

Craig Raine

Atlantic Books
LONDON

First published in Great Britain in hardback in 2011 by
Atlantic Books, an imprint of Atlantic Books Ltd.

Copyright © Craig Raine, 2010

The moral right of Craig Raine to be identified as the author
of this work has been asserted by him in accordance with the
Copyright, Designs and Patents Act of 1988.

All rights reserved. No part of this publication may be
reproduced, stored in a retrieval system or transmitted in any
form or by any means, electronic, mechanical, photocopying,
recording or otherwise, without the prior permission of both the
copyright owner and the above publisher of this book.

10 9 8 7 6 5 4 3 2 1

*A CIP catalogue record for this book is available
from the British Library.*

ISBN: 978 1 84887 285 1

Printed in the UK by CPI William Clowes Beccles NR34 7TL

Atlantic Books
An imprint of Atlantic Books Ltd
Ormond House
26–27 Boswell Street
London WC1N 3JZ

www.atlantic-books.co.uk

Contents

How Snow Falls   1

I Remember My Mother Dying   2

Rashomon   24

In Hospital   35

Night   38

La Médica Harkevitch   41

Three Poems after Willem Van Toorn   46

Words Upon the Window Pane   50

A Festive Poem for Albie Marber   52

51 Ways to Lose a Balloon   55

Ars Poetica   61

Venice   66

Those No-Doubt-About-It Infidelity Blues   70

Davos Documentary B & W   75

L. F. Rosen: Three Poems   77

Marcel's Fancy-Dress Party   81

High Table   84

For Pat Kavanagh   120

On the Slopes   121

A la recherche du temps perdu   125

Acknowledgements   167

How Snow Falls

Like the unshaven prickle
of a sharpened razor,

this new coldness in the air,
the pang

of something intangible.
Filling our eyes,

the sinusitis of perfume
without the perfume.

And then love's vertigo,
love's exactitude,

this snow, this transfiguration
we never quite get over.

I Remember My Mother Dying

I remember
we were driving to my father's funeral. An overcast day.
A downcast day. Outside Darlington, eight miles away,

my ten-year-old son Vaska asked: Do you think
your brother will try to murder you? My cock shrank.

I remember
my father's open coffin in the unlit dining room.
White nostril hairs, fog-lights in the gloom.

His face was the colour
of old glazed cheddar.

His right eyelid was straining open,
to see what was going to happen:

stitches stretched the parchment
like the flysheet of a tent.

It was the face of someone about to be shot,
about to flinch away from being hit,

apprehensive as those Hungarian security police,
all their body language a single plea,

snapped by that *Life* magazine photographer
John Sadovy, just as the trigger

was pulled in Budapest in 1956.
I felt faintly sick.

But I had to think about the speech
my brother had just asked me to make in church.

I remember
that my mother had found a phrase,
empty, sentimental, formulaic self-praise,

something to say, to explain why
my father's corpse was on display.

She repeated it to everyone
as they offered their commiserations.

She was playing the indomitable wife:
'I looked after him all his life

and I wasn't going to let anyone else
look after him now.' Pure pretence.

She went along with it, but the whole stupid idea
had my brother's wonky, macabre steer.

I remember
the funeral congregation
paying wary attention

to my brother's affected upper-gloss voice
pledging to care for my mother. His solemn promise.

Three years later,
he turned up from god knows where

and terrorized the middle-aged female wardens,
issuing edicts, insults and orders,

a rip-tide of abuse by telephone
every night and all night long.

It was a little freehold flat in sheltered housing.
My mother began to lose her mind.

I remember
my brother, drunk, as usual,
announcing his 3.30 a.m. arrival

by leaning on my front doorbell.
And shouting through the letterbox as well.

'I've brought you my mother's ashes.'
The ineffectual, thirty-second thrashing

I gave him was a surprise to me.
I was hampered by my nudity,

my bare feet, my open dressing gown –
and he cycled shakily off to Summertown.

I don't think he was expecting me to spurn
the sturdy screw-top bronze plastic urn.

I remember
seeing my brother on a bench,
sweaty, unshaven, intense,

his tight tie-knot shiny with dirt,
the morning after our mother died.

It was outside the Radcliffe Hospital.
He was talking to himself, spraying spittle

like a madman. I laughed out loud.
Because he'd been abusive, he wasn't allowed

to see my mother's body in the morgue.
He was reviewing the legal arguments,

taking legal advice,
raising his voice…

Undertakers, not one but *two* firms,
had already refused to deal with him.

In the end, though, he put her on display
just like my father, for a couple of days.

I remember
the first inkling of my mother's mental decline
was a disagreement about the design

of plastic cocoa-butter containers,
which, against all evidence, she maintained

had a *hidden* pump, something recessed,
that would spring up when pressed.

I remember,
when she took out her top set of teeth
at Sunday lunch, facing the truth

that something was seriously wrong.
Her wincing delicacy was always so strong

she would berate
my father for removing his dental plate

to rinse out a painful raspberry pip,
'in public', under our kitchen tap.

Sometimes when criticized, he'd jut out
his bottom set,

his whole face a grotesque leer,
and ask for 'a gottle of geer',

like a ventriloquist's dummy –
his routine routine, no longer funny.

I remember
at the same lunch, my mother said:
'I'm dying' and added:

'At least there's the flat.
You'll make money on that.'

Just the two of us. The words were humble,
but her voice was slightly trembling.

It was a declaration of love, disguised
for her other difficult, distant son, as pure prose.

I remember
as I helped her into her black coat,
she asked me, 'Am I all right?'

I remember
that I didn't want to frighten her,
so I said, 'Of course you are.'

And I straightened the turquoise brooch
on her right lapel and watched her fingers search

for the chipped gilt buttons, one by one,
as her blind eyes darkly searched for mine.

'You're my protector.'
Too late, I put my arms too late around her.

I remember
that every Sunday I made her her favourite drink,
lemonade and Advocaat, simple pub plonk.

When she became worried about her mind,
she stopped drinking the Snowballs. Another sign.

I remember
her trying to remember. After she died,
we found Post-it notes with names to memorize.

HAROLD PINTER. OLIVE WALKER.
Then 1 2 3 4. Then 1 2 3. Then 1 2 3 4.

I remember
asking questions to test her, and her strategies,
her desperate remedies:

'How old was your father
when he got married?' Answer:

'*My mother never wanted me.*'
Question: 'Was he 40? Was he 30?'

 A favourite all-purpose answer:
'*When I had my operation for cancer*

there was blood all over my back.'
Or a variant on 'Jack Sprat',

a nursery rhyme,
but also a feat in her private scheme:

Jack Sprat could eat no fat,
His wife could eat no lean,

But with a drop of HP Sauce
They licked the platter clean.

I remember
another scrap of verse
that represented Annapurna, F6, Everest:

Salvation Army, free from sin,
All go to heaven in a corned-beef tin.

I remember
that before she became ill
my mother had a dark-eyed, frail

wispy delicacy, a gracefulness
created by her partial sight loss.

She would stand,
smiling, unseeing, with folded hands.

When her brain began to struggle
and fail, she became ugly.

Her nose got bigger.
Everything was coarser.

Under her eyes, the bags
were great wax seals, swags

on a medieval document.
I felt an irresistible instinct:

I wanted to wash my hands when I left her flat,
as if I'd just been to the toilet.

I remember
my mother's instincts were better
than mine. Her sense of etiquette

survived the indignity of being on the loo:
'Excuse me.' She said 'thank you'

at the end of even the briefest visit.
Her manners went on being exquisite.

I remember
trying to get her to drink
a mouthful or two of milk.

I was worried in case she lost
her swallow reflex. She'd started to fast

and she was losing weight at speed.
Her: 'Can I lie down?' Me:

'Yes, when you've drunk the milk.'
This is the small talk

we make when someone is dying.
She takes a sip, then lies back sighing

on her pillows. I stroke her hair.
She moans, continuously, lying there.

Her: 'Can I lie down now?' Pretending to scoff,
Me: 'You *are* lying down.' She laughs.

I remember
this resourceful *viva voce* between her
and Dr Duodo, the hospital doctor,

the afternoon she was admitted
to the Radcliffe Infirmary. He said,

'Do you know where you are?'
'Yes.' 'Well, can you tell me where

that is?' 'It's here.' 'But where are you?'
'I'm sitting up in bed.' 'Where are you

sitting up in bed?' 'Well, here.' 'Where is here?'
'In bed.' She was sitting in an armchair…

I remember
the details of the diagnosis.
After a week of tests, Dr Duodo told us

that her mental decline was the result
of low sodium and haemoglobin counts.

That the weight loss had been stopped.
With two pounds gained, she was in better shape.

Her sodium level had been raised
from 120 to 130. Dr Duodo was pleased,

but it needed to settle down
at about 135, 140, or somewhere between.

A brain scan showed atrophy
in places, some calcification, but no pathology,

so the decline could be reversed
if she was properly nursed

and stayed in hospital.
(My brother was all

for nursing her himself, at home.)
Her anti-depressants lowered the sodium

so different types should be tried.
The ultrasound needed to be clarified:

it was difficult to assess
in the area of the pancreas.

Dr Duodo was arranging a CAT scan.
'We will do everything we can.'

I remember
thinking the signet ring on his little finger
was like the band on a cigar,

then thinking I've read that before,
in Christopher Reid's first book somewhere…

I remember
the CAT scan showed no pancreatitis.
Instead the diagnosis

was cancer of the stomach wall,
nothing beyond as yet, but clearly fatal.

We refused the offer of an endoscopy
as intrusive and unnecessary.

Her chest infection was worse but antibiotics
would probably do the trick…

I remember
sitting in the hospital cafeteria
reading aloud to my wife from *Granta*:

Best of Young British Novelists,
snorting with laughter and ripping the piss

out of Philip Hensher's High-Table prose.
Two tables away, a girl used

a CD from her Discman as a mirror
to put on her eyeliner.

I remember
Zadie Smith's story
as the best thing in the anthology.

(I had plenty of time for bedside reading,
while I listened for my mother's snagged breathing.)

The story is subtly semi-allegorical.
Two different passions are held in parallel –

terrorists who are fanatical
have a snowball fight; a sturdy black girl

is heartbroken over a photograph.
In both cases it's blind faith

to an absolute inner conviction.
Appearances conceal the turmoil within.

The photo shows two people with noses
sellotaped like pigs to their faces…

I remember
my mother's own description of herself:
'I'm more bewildered than anything else.'

Me: 'If you can use a word like *bewildered*,
you can't be that bewildered. It's a good word.'

Her [laughing]: 'I've got lots in my head, don't worry.'
Me: 'And you make jokes. You're funny.'

Her: 'Where are you without a sense of humour?'
Or with it? Bewildered. Staving off stupor.

I remember
Eileen in the bed next to my mother.
Most of the time, she kept up a whimper.

A wardrobe had fallen on her,
trapping her leg against a radiator:

for twelve hours, it cooked,
until the flesh was completely baked.

My mother looked across
(her new anti-depressant and the glucose

were kicking in: chemical euphoria
after a haemorrhage caused by her cancer)

and loudly remarked,
'I don't think *she's* going to make it.'

I remember
Isaac looked at her glucose drip
and said it lacked a fairground goldfish.

I remember
my mother complaining her lips were dry.
Sister brought her orange juice to try.

She stirred her finger in the juice
and pulled a face:

'It isn't even cooked.'
Sister [sagely]: 'If you read it in a book,

you wouldn't believe it, would you?
You couldn't make it up, could you?'

I remember
strange moments of lucidity.
I asked her how she'd slept. 'Rather fitfully.'

I told her I'd been to a reading by actors
of a play by Nina [my daughter]:

'For a play, I think realism is
the only sound basis.'

I had never heard her say
anything so confident until that day.

I remember
teasing her about her hearing aid.
'The whole thing's a charade,'

I said, 'we talked without it
for at least ten minutes.

No, don't pretend: you understood
everything *before* I found it in the bed.

You've been *pretending* all these years
that you couldn't hear:

it was the ear jewellery you were after.'
She exploded with laughter,

spraying milk out of her mouth.
For her, she was mildly uncouth

when I said I'd put the thing back in her ear.
'Well, I didn't think you were

going to put it in my bottom.'
A reconfiguration of her very atoms.

I remember
she thought she was in the infirmary
for somebody else. So she could have their baby.

I remember
the surgeons in their scrubs
looking like pirates. Olive-green drab.

I remember
two days before she died, a question:
would I pluck the hairs out of her chin?

There were none on the ward,
so I bought some tweezers down the road.

Every time a hair was plucked,
she sighed, almost like someone being slowly fucked.

Yes, she said, yes. *Yes.*
The last pleasures of the flesh.

It was sensual and very intimate.
And she let me share it.

I remember
as I plucked the last,
she asked me where my brother was.

'He's gone to watch the racing on TV.'
She, eyes shut, amused: 'Has he?

Has he now? The *rat*.'
Amused, eyes shut.

I remember
the ripple mattress creaking like packed snow.
It moved to prevent bedsores.

I remember
that watching her go
seemed a process so slow

it was like watching the candles burn
out on the Christmas tree. Blue uncertain

faltering buds of light
out to sea on a starless night,

disappearing,
re-appearing.

I remember
two stages towards death:
the first was when her false teeth

looked like false teeth,
clicking, loose in her mouth.

The second was when
a kind of beauty returned:

pallor and purity, one grain of rice.
Her lips were pale, picked out, precise.

I remember
that dead she was the colour
of a beeswax candle, her mouth a horror,

in shock, her bloody lips
wide open, vampiric, chapped.

The oxygen was still in her nose
like a butterfly's proboscis.

I remember
the way the nurses folded the bottom sheet
over her face and over her feet

like Danish pastry in the shape of a kite.
Down and across. Left and then right.

They secured the finished shape
with 'Magic' invisible Sellotape.

It was a procedure and a rhythmic ritual.
They double-taped the string of her label.

I remember
the slewed plastic doors
slumped on their hinges down the corridors,

the terrible art on the walls.

I remember
being surprised the dead didn't look peaceful.

I remember
heaped ashtrays at every entrance,
surrounded by patients

puffing away in pyjamas and dressing gowns.
Fag ends balanced everywhere, thick on the ground.

I remember
getting into the bed with my mother
so I could hold her. So I could hold her.

And I remember
that the numbers on the key-pad
on the pay-phone just outside the ward

were gone, blank as a bar of chocolate,
overused, obliterate…

Rashomon

THE BANDIT, TAJOMARU

We had a chance encounter on the Yamashina road.
His wife was seated sideways on the horse.

He held the bridle in his sunburnt hand and walked.
Her veil was lifted briefly by the breeze.

I saw her face and fell in love.
She had a mole beside her mouth,

a drop of Indian ink still wet.
I could have killed the husband there and then.

Saki at blood temperature, or blood itself –
to someone like me it's all the same.

I've been a bandit all my life.
I have my thirsts to quench.

But somehow I decided otherwise this day.
Perhaps because the Yamashina road can be a busy road.

I told the husband there was treasure in the grove.
A buried hoard of bullion, beryl, lapis lazuli.

The Samurai believed my tale of treasure trove.
She waited with the horse while we forced through the cane.

I overpowered him and tied him up.
The cords cut into his kimono.

He was trussed up like a caterpillar writhing.
The gag was tight and made him look a toothless crone.

I told her he was taken sick
and led her gently by the hand into the grove.

The bamboo squeezed itself against her flesh
as if the place itself were passionate.

Her hat came off. Her hair came down.
The place was plucking at her clothes.

When she saw her husband bound,
her hand slid out of mine and drew a dagger.

She was angry. I was amused but agile.
Struck, the dagger went out like a light.

I worked my knee between her legs.
Shantung. Hirsute. Digging, digging deep,

I worked the seam. But when I came to go,
she begged, her hair across her mouth,

that one of us should die. I or her husband.
So that her shame should not be known to both.

Whoever won the fight would take her for his wife.
The husband rubbed his untied arms.

Our swords unsheathed like shantung silk when torn
and after seven strokes the Samurai was dead,

his last long moan a sigh of satisfaction.
But when I turned, the girl was gone.

Her hand in mine was very small.
I ask this court the supreme penalty.

THE WIFE, MASAGO

I was only nineteen years old, O holy father.
We had been married seven happy months.

26

When he had used me for his lust and left,
his open blue kimono billowing behind,

I turned to where my husband was tied up.
The gag pulled down the corners of his mouth

so that his face was tragic, a Kabuki mask.
I did not recognize his stranger's eyes.

I searched for tears trembling there
to match the mirage in my own

that made the bamboo curtain faint.
And grow upright again. And faint.

Seeing the hatred in my husband's eyes,
I rearranged my robe to cover this dishonoured flesh.

I said with broken, mended, broken voice:
Takejiro, husband, we cannot live like this.

You saw my shame. And now your nostrils smell my shame.
I am defiled forever and so we both must die.

I will kill you first and then myself.
The expression in my husband's eyes agreed.

Then I saw my dagger shining like the evening star,
uncertain, tearful, on the grass, a million miles away.

I think I said: Takejiro, give me your life.
And I pushed the blade quite easily

like cream cheese left to harden overnight outside.
I must have fainted. I woke up on the forest floor,

old cedar needles like cinnamon next to my eyes.
Takejiro had gone to kiss his ancestors on both cheeks.

But then I couldn't kill myself
because the life in me was strong, too strong to die.

I stabbed my throat and lived.
I threw myself into a lake

but felt my body fight for breath on shore.
I hanged myself and was rescued by my hands.

I am only nineteen, father, holy father.
It will take a life to die of shame.

THE HUSBAND, TAKEJIRO, THROUGH A MEDIUM

Masago with a mole beside her mouth,
Brown, the shiny sepia of apple seed.

When he had finished with her flesh,
he held her hand and whispered words of comfort.

I wanted to cry across the grove:
Do not believe this bandit, love.

He said: Your husband will hate you now.
He said: Leave your husband, marry me.

Her fingers played among the cedar needles.
As if her other hand belonged to him,

he traced the lines of life and love and fate.
His finger walked the paths across her palm.

And then my wife, Masago, agreed to go with him.
We had been married only seven months.

I watched the mole move by her mouth
as my Masago said: But you must kill him now.

I cannot be your wife while he still lives.
He stood up, transfixed, then struck her down.

He came bowlegged across the grove.
His cock in its ruff of hair

was exactly at the level of my eyes.
He said: Shall I kill her, or shall I let her live?

For these words I plead that he be pardoned.
I hesitated. Masago with that mole.

I hesitated and she fled beyond his reach.
He took my sword, my bow and arrows,

cut one cord and left without another word.
As I untied my other bonds, I heard someone weeping.

Gradually, this weeping came closer, closer,
until I realized that it was I.

I took Masago's dagger from the forest floor,
wiped it clean and stabbed myself.

I was there forever while the darkness came.
Night came like a woman's hair over my face.

The stars shone up above like dagger points.
The blood was cold and hard as frozen snow.

At dawn someone I could not see crept in the grove
and drew the dagger out and blood was bitter in my mouth.

THE WOODCUTTER

Your honour, I was chopping wood.
My right hand slid from head to haft.

Sweet cedar chips were spurting in the gloom like sparks.
The Yamashina road was five hundred yards away.

The head of the axe worked loose.
I stopped and stooped to wedge it tight.

And then I heard a harness creak.
I heard the clink of bit.

I heard the horse's breath.
But bamboo canes came thick between.

I could not see. I saw the aftermath.
A grove of trampled grass

and a body in a blue kimono.
Dead from a single sword wound in the chest.

A bluebottle was walking in the thin-lipped wound.
Shantung. Hirsute. Beryl. Lapis lazuli.

There was a coil of cord.
Can I leave the court, your excellency?

I am a poor peasant, lord.
Firs are waiting to be felled.

ENSEMBLE: BANDIT, WIFE, HUSBAND, WOODCUTTER

I killed her husband with my father's father's sword.
The seventh stroke.

Where his kimono parted when he took a breath,
there I pushed the dagger slowly in.

I took the dagger she had dropped
and drove it into my dishonoured heart.

I untied the husband's bonds and beat him in fair fight.
He fell, both hands bleeding where he held the sword.

His look of loathing was a clear demand for death.
Give me your life and I will follow like a shadow at your heels.

I tried to sacrifice myself so many different ways.
But bodies are not brutes you drive into the abattoir.

I wished to ride her as a rider rides a horse
in battle. Selfishly. Unthinking. Harsh.

I was chopping wood.
No. My right hand slid from head to haft.

Sweet cedar chips like sparks.
No. My seed was spurting in the gloom like sparks.

I was really after buried treasure.
I was after complicated pleasure:

to violate the girl before her spouse,
this way, that way, in front, behind, without a pause.

Soon the other's breath will fight for breath,
the reek of rope around his neck.

Between his legs a heavy saddle
and an upward curving pommel.

It was the mole beside her mouth.
It made me realize that love is not a myth.

He rode his mount into the ground,
till she was broken, saddled, reined.

My heart was ripped like shantung silk.
I felt each fibre break

and slowly tear the tear across.
Whatever happened happened to the missing horse.

The heart of darkness tolling, tolling.
Seven strokes and stopped.

Cold air of evening and fingers feeling for the dagger
when they find my soul and fling it far from me.

In Hospital

(after Pasternak)

A crowd blocked the pavement,
jostling like shoppers at the sales.
The stretcher slid into position,
the ambulance let out a long wail.

Cheekbones, check curtains, Cheka:
stills from the outstripped street.
The nurse undid her smelling salts
and swayed on the jump seat.

A drainpipe gargled. The storm
slashed and the hospital clerk
took out a fresh admission form
and filled in every section.

There was no bed free in the ward
so they arranged a mattress on the floor.
The draught from the windows stirred
weak poltergeists of iodine.

Turbulent treetops and sky
were framed in the window frame.
The new patient studied the floorboards,
saw suitcases under the beds nearby.

Struck by the Sister's urgency,
her oblivious, concentrated face,
he realized his little adventure
might run down in this run-down place.

Gratitude surprised him.
A wall outside remembered
Proust's patch of wall,
throbbing like an ember.

Buildings began to glow
and burst into flames.
He watched a maple branch
making an awkward bow.

And he thought: this is just,
perfect, this is exactly right –
Bergotte's wall, these iron beds,
dying in the dead of night.

But this analgesic is bitter,
it brings tears to my eyes.
As I try to find my handkerchief,
God's purpose goes awry.

In the shadow of the valley of beds,
life, I know, is a gift –
a gift that I somehow mislaid
when my attention began to drift.

Your hands are ablaze
with diamonds in the dark.
Like a jeweller, Lord,
closing up a ring in its case.

Night

(after Pasternak)

Without lingering,
night begins to lighten and lift
as the pilot lifts
above the drowsing day

and dwindles in mist,
lost in the midst of light,
like the tiny cross
of a laundry mark,

leaving behind the all-night bars
in strange towns, sentry-go,
stokers, steam engines, stations –
all striking their spark.

The shadow of his aircraft
a silent skier on the cloud below.
And all the crowded stars
disperse in all directions,

strewn like the Milky Way
as everything suddenly banks.
Headlands shine out
over uncertain horizons.

The boiler house furnace flares
in the stoker's stare.
In Paris, Mars and Venus
stoop to the street,

where a glistening poster
is pasted for the Opéra.
High up, at a window
wide ajar on a mansard roof,

this sleepless soul
hypnotizes the far horizon.
He stares at the stars
as though they were the troubles

that kept him awake,
a constellation of cares.
Don't go to sleep. Work.
Work. Don't go to sleep.

Like a pilot, like a planet,
don't give way to drowsiness, poet.
You are the pledge we give eternity
and so the slave of every second.

La Médica Harkevitch

At 6 in the morning,
the telephone tells us you are dead.

Instead of mourning,
I prefer to think of you alive –

tortoise mouth, orange-peel pores,
your legs like bolsters.

The *dottoressa*, giving us pause,
years ago: new hairstyle already wilted,

your evening gown a comfit,
enrobed in hundreds and thousands,

your medical medal kitsch, no comfort,
a decorative decoration – singular

in all its encrusted splendour,
and impossible to arrange satisfactorily.

It was semiprecious plunder,
a giant suspender only just

clinging to your steep chest,
the slippery slope where talc curdled

between each chaste
braced breast. You were drenched

and the bathroom looked like a cement works.
The beau monde, fashionable life –

basking in black tie, socialite sharks –
bored you and scared you to death.

That August heat. A mechanic's chest
like a Jackson Pollock. The tilde's heatwave.

Roadside rocks in veils. Heat. He checks
the oil, like a matador. Dry heat.

———————

Last Easter, we hoped you were dying.
You were bedridden, gaga, unable to move,

so Li decided it was time to fly in
and say goodbye at your bedside, to sit

in silence, just holding your hand.
In fact, you pushed her hand away.

Repeatedly. You needed the bed-pan.
In private. A tiny sign you were there.

The nurse came. Li left the room,
then returned to sit in the stench.

But she had come with a gift, a *rhume*,
so that her nose was blocked. To shit or scent.

Your right ear was swollen and sore
where you tended to tilt your head.

Your right eye saw what it saw
through the saline tail

from the tear duct
into the opposite, encrusted corner.

The left eye saw nothing, ducked
nothing, a blue unblinking circle.

At the edge of your face and hairline,
bran-coloured coins, little blotches,

like cabin windows on an airliner.
Otherwise your skin was sallow and clear.

Not toothless, but no bottom set,
so your face had collapsed.

It wasn't the silence. Li was upset
by your unwavering

stare at the ceiling, and she said:
How is it you don't blink?

And immediately you answered
by closing your eyes.

And after another hour,
you spoke one word in Russian:

Dura. A last drop from a dusty ewer.
Which means 'idiot' in English.

Shaking her head, Li said 'no',
when she was able to speak.

'I'm the Lisa you know,
who loves you very much.' Silence.

But then you pressed
her hand, made your mouth make a kiss.

Its laminates compressed,
the bow was strung with waxed cord.

Atoms on the inside were crushed,
outside atoms were lonely.

Released, they rushed
away and together.

And the arrow found the flesh
ready to sheathe its sharpness.

Sschuu. Its arrow flash
a sneeze. Eros doubling Azrael.

Dasvidanye – you said. Like an afrit
you were gone. Carried away. Swept off your feet.

Three Poems after Willem Van Toorn

FALLOW LAND

The view is clean as cartridge paper
freshly pinned to a drawing board.
But marks long to emerge
and the eye searches for something.
Under the sand, you sense
the divine dirt of a pencil point.

The artist's fingers are just out of frame.
Only water, water and sand,
and a frisson of grass at the fringe.
Creation, containing creation –
upheaval's hosanna to the only human.

[In the distance, dim ideas,
patiently waiting
for vision to make them visible.]

TRANSLATION

I

Again the fields are strange with frost.
The vivid odours of September, October.
He arranges the last things he saw
between the farmyard and the horizon:
a jinking hare, the printed dew;
the patch of bald earth

where nothing ever grew;
the hunter's track deep into the polder,
studied for almost a hundred years;
the orchard's secret baby owls.
The earth he ploughed with horses
all his life. He knows it like his skin.
He laughs as the morning opens in his mind.

II

He is lost, lost in the housing estate,
lost for words to tell his horses
he is powerless to pass
beyond these buildings
that thwart him like a dream.
He wants a piss, shielded
by the willow. Which knows him.
Which has disappeared.

The kind young women who live here now
find him in their gardens.
They take him home, his old eyes
troubled like a two year old.
'He was standing near the hedge.'
The emptiness falls
through his head like manna.

Again he hears the childhood promise:
'I will take you back. Back to *melk en honing*.'

HOUSE

You knew exactly where you were:
white string stretched along the foundations.
Eye contact with the spirit level
told you the walls were true.
Work table. Bed. Clean sheets.

But the blueprint blurs
in its portfolio. Under the floors,
grass writhes like albino wiring.
Take a look over your shoulder,

back there at the beginning,
and watch what was once so solid
give up the ghost. Walls so thin
the world shines through.

Your house existed before it was built.
All its detail was a dream.
Without love can perfection endure?

The idea is always eternal.
But not what we make of it.
Worn treads. Cramped corridors. A glory hole.
The gentle tick of time abrades even brick,
will wear away stone. Bet on it.

Words Upon the Window Pane

Your husband gone, as gone as the dead,
but without any sadness, thinning your lips.

And the view from the rectory, scratched,
scratched longwise, scratched slantwise,

almost scratched out by continual rain,
and scratched on the window, two words,

saying all of somebody's childhood:
always raining. Forever this.

Love, death, adventure, life –
staring at print and wet twigs

and the tic of redcurrant leaves.
Romance a semicolon sitting side saddle.

Two grooves in the grassy lane
go nowhere, a vapour trail losing itself in mist.

Once for all, this ten-year-old girl,
making herself dizzy, like radar

alone at the end of a runway.
So what is the use of my saying

the glass is thick with moons,
with bison herds of meteorite,

with comets in their wedding trains?
Why contradict your deepest conviction

that what was shining is scratched,
when between the bars of your balcony

there is fog on five cobwebs,
fresh as a set of fingerprints?

A Festive Poem for Albie Marber

This is the saga
Of Albie Marber
And the twinkle in his eye.

Albie Marber
Strolled round the harbour,
Watching the ships go by.

Albie Marber
Snoozed in the arbour,
Sucking his mother dry.

Albie Marber,
Snug in his Barbour,
Keeping his nappy dry.

Albie Marber
Ransacked the larder
Searching for pecan pie.

Albie Marber
Got harder and harder –
Had to unbutton his fly.

Albie Marber
Sat by the Aga,
Smelling the bacon fry.

Albie Marber,
Tossing the caber,
Won without seeming to try.

Albie Marber
Hated the barber –
Not that we'll ever know why.

Albie Marber,
Driving his Lada
(the Skoda was priced too high).

Albie Marber
Greeted his neighbour
Eyeing her ass on the sly.

Albie Marber
Went into labour,
Forcing a fart to fly.

Albie Marber
Wanted to scarper
Whenever a bore dropped by.

Albie Marber
Shouted blue murder
And ordered a shot of red-eye.

Albie Marber
Sat in the parlour
Eating his curds and why?

Albie Marber
And Andreas Baader
Never saw eye to eye.

Albie Marber
Sang in the *Stabat Mater*
And his voice was trebly high.

Albie Marber
Went into purdah
Whenever a poet came by…

51 Ways to Lose a Balloon

Here is your balloon. Heart-shaped, hard with helium, filled from an iron cigar. It has more creases than your baby sister's arm.

Be careful. There are 51 ways to lose a balloon.

1. You taste your ear wax for the very first time and…

2. Your mother is shopping. For no particular reason, you are staring at an egg box in the grocer's window, when it suddenly occurs to you how much it looks like a caterpillar and…

3. The string of your balloon feels like the light-string in the lavatory. So you pull it once and let it go…

4. Your baby brother's sandal comes off. He's being difficult and bunches up his foot. You give him the balloon to hold and…

5. Your baby brother's sandal comes off. He isn't being difficult. He doesn't squirm away. But you notice that the sole of the sandal looks exactly like a crinkle-cut crisp and…

6. You think you want to pop your balloon, so you get a pin and scratch it. It pops before you have properly decided.

7. At the last second, you only just avoid stepping into a helping of dog pooh and…

8. As you walk around the zoo, you notice that the sleeves of all the penguins' dinner jackets are too long. (That's why you *never* see their hands.) You notice that some of the penguins are in for the sack race. And that the leopard is disguised as a ripe banana. You look at the tiger's war paint. You watch the vulture fold and unfold its wings just like your father getting cross with his map. And you think how the gorilla looks like a bee, only without any wings, and that one of the tropical fish breathes like the nail clippers at home. And sometime, you couldn't say when, your balloon has gone.

9. You are practising your cough and curling your tongue and get carried away and…

10. Your uncle tickles you under the arm that is holding the balloon and…

11. You are writing your name on your balloon when the nib goes through…

12. There is a standpipe in the garden. You switch it on louder and splash your shoes and…

13. Brown, with dabs of red and gold. A scrap of litter caught on the lilac. Maybe a Mars Bar. You reach to tidy it up when it taxies like an aeroplane and turns into a butterfly and…

14. Somehow, holding your balloon is like holding your breath and in the end you have to let go…

15. You see a bicycle being eaten by the boot of a car and…

16. You step on a wobbly paving stone and it pees in your shoe
    – very cold, as it is when you wake in the morning – and…

17. Your mother ties it tightly to your wrist. But you are worried
    about whether the blood can get to your fingers, so you scrape
    it off and…

18. You notice that your shoes are on the wrong feet and…

19. You get a 10p piece out from a difficult pocket under your
    raincoat to pop in the woman's Oxfam tin and…

20. You are poking the fingers of your free hand down your throat,
    for the pleasure of going *krrgh*, when your mouth suddenly
    fills with sick and…

21. The cat is as warm as a tea-cosy on your lap when she
    suddenly switches on her claws and…

22. You see an oily in the gutter and…

23. You know you are going to sneeze and you start feeling
    frantically for a handkerchief and…

24. You have sneezed and now you're busy looking for where it
    went and…

25. You watch the sea trying to stand up. But it always falls down,
    until you forget what is there in your hand…

26. A wasp won't leave you alone even though you do some dance
    steps. Then it settles on your hand so you can see its handlebar
    eyebrows and how nervous its bottom is and…

27. Your dad is cross with your mum for losing her car-keys again. A tear plips into her handbag like a tiddlywink. So you start to cry and…

28. Your mum is cross with your brother – for something *you* did – so you start to smile and…

29. You had your eyedrops two hours ago (three in each eye) and now is the moment they come down the back of your nose…

30. You see a cyclist cycling by with a bunch of bananas protecting his head and…

31. You want to do a wee and have to hang on with both your hands…

32. Your little brother is playing the banjo with your tennis racket. When you twist it out of his hands…

33. You come off the beach barefoot to buy an ice cream and step on a cigarette end…

34. You have picked your nose and rolled up a stretchy bit into a ball. It won't flick off, so you put the string of your balloon under your arm…

35. You get a little electric shock from a bunch of nettles and…

36. There's a friendly dog in the street who jumps up at your face like someone playing netball…

37. You are sitting on the teapot lid when you see that the horrible tramp asleep on the bench has just woken up…

38. Someone has made a smell. You don't want people to think it is you, so you wave your arms about and...

39. *Fiddley-pom, fiddley-pom.* You are doing a chant in the garden when your teacher leans over the fence to say hello and...

40. Your big brother has left one of his football boots out on the lawn. It reminds you of something, but you can't think what. It just lies there teasing you. You turn away and then spin round, trying to take it by surprise. You screw up your eyes. You look slightly to the left. You look without thinking. Something to do with the studs. A pig! It's a sow on her side and...

41. *Tug. Tug.* You can feel how badly the balloon wants to be off on its own and finally you feel so sorry for it that...

42. It goes soft and tired and shrivelled and old like fruit or like grandma.

43. You see a fig in the sky and then another fig and then...

44. You are out for a walk. The conkers are everywhere, like a minefield. Naturally, you tiptoe through the danger, when one of the conkers smacks to pieces in front of your feet...

45. The wind from a 125 whips it out of your hand...

46. You see a bubble car. It's like watching someone driving a poached egg and you start to laugh and...

47. It's that horrible man from next door, doing a peep-oh over his garden wall...

48. You are making a list in your head of the birthday presents you want, and you can still feel the string in your hand after you notice your balloon has gone.

49. Your mum makes you give it to a little girl in a wheelchair.

50. When you go to sleep, the balloon changes into a tulip and goes out to grow in the garden...

51. This is the way no one ever warns you about...

Ars Poetica

Listen to this. You hold to my ear
your bottle of Coca-Cola. *Listen.*

Barely audible. The idea of an idea.
The first, far mosquito, holding its note,
perfecting its pitch, at the furthest edge.
Near. Far. Nowhere. There.
I think. I say:

a Coke with tinnitus.

You nod. *Exactly.* The yes of writers.
The nod we give exactitude. And you say,
Don't you miss that? Poetry?

I say: the image won't work.
A Coke with tinnitus
is enigmatic out of context.

Poetry has to be love at first sight.
Obvious and impossible.
Ideal. Unhesitating. It strikes you straightaway.

For example: fir cones like faeces,
at the base of each tree.

It isn't an arranged marriage –
although of course it is arranged,
arranged to look like love at first sight.

II

I think of my son Isaac in New York,
designing dresses for Diane von Furstenberg,
pinning poems on his model:
Mallarmé's *pli selon pli*,
the momentum of material,
the way a curve can seem inevitable,
the fall of a fold.

One long night. Another.
We are waiting till it feels exact,
ruthless till we feel the fit.

And then we edit out the working.
No invitation for wonderful wordy Henry James.
Creation is conclusive.
After an infinity of adjustments.

For example, avoiding obvious finality:
at the base of each tree,
fir cones like faeces.
You have to hear the difference.

III

It is a kind of choreography.
We work with what we've got,
until we work it out,
until it's right. And what is 'right'?

Balanchine's muse was Suzanne Farrell:
five foot six and a half on the street
but six foot one on stage.
Poetry: language on point.

IV

I will always be married to poetry, I say,
but I have fallen in love with prose.
I am excited by prose
because I do not know exactly what it is.

And this late poem is written by a man
hopelessly in love with prose at 65.
Bringing danger and discoveries
back to the marital bed.

(In return for the things
he has taken to prose
from the marital bed.)

v

In the course of one April afternoon,
the upswept, blow-dried,
lacquered, highlighted magnolia,
magnificent as Mrs Thatcher,
coiffure a blazing candelabra,

this magnolia parts with its petals
as if by a course of chemo.

And the ground is treacherous
as a wet toilet on a train,
used pink toilet paper underfoot,
rusty, broken, dark with decay.

VI

It strikes you straightaway
and what it means.

An earthquake of Lego.
A litter of letters.
A Babel of bricks.

VII

Which brings me back to poetry.
Like meeting an old girlfriend:
awkward at first, but also familiar,
both familiar and forgotten.

And I can hear something new,
there at the edge of the farthest edge,
something faint and fugitive,
shy as the tinnitus of Coke.

Venice

(for Rosemary Goad)

At the Lido,
weak waves, taking their time.
A sea with emphysema.

Venice: that sinking feeling, Rose,
as another indifferent, passionate poem
is visited on *la Serenissima*.

At least I own a mortgage here.
Opposite the Naval Museum,
next to a canal, clean and tidal.

They're hand-faking antiques
in the workshop across the way,
brushes khaki with pollen, varnish.

You can see the seethe of air
over the glue pot
on their Camping Gaz.

I sit in the warm shade,
shelling walnuts,
and face the lagoon

outside my own front door,
watching the world go by –
sometimes in sections.

Twice a day – usually 6 in the morning,
or 6 in the evening –
the house has a heart attack:

a liner heading for the open sea,
blocking the view like a tower block.
Bang up to your eye.

Minutes pass as it passes,
passengers in excelsis,
like a Stanley Spencer resurrection.

The whole ship a thunder-sheet,
sounding her cargo of decibels,
shivering our timbers,

leaving hairline cracks in the plaster,
making waves
trip over the quayside moulding.

On grey days, foghorns,
gondolas drunk at their moorings,
launches laden with shopping bags.

Mosquito nets of rain.
The canal thrashing
like a catch of tuna

and afterwards a glossy dark green.
Succeeded by sunshine,
by a bumptious speedboat

on its fizzing short fuse,
by the Navy launch,
its wallowing wake a loofah of foam.

Solid shadows.
Then indeterminate dusk,
then darkness

then something far out to sea,
a vulgar diamanté brooch.
I love the waiters going home,

bow ties undone,
like a pair of shades
in their fly-fronted shirts.

This walnut kernel – gilded bronze,
rococo turns, carved flourishes –
I hold it in my fingers,

turn it to catch the light,
a tiny pair
of antique angel wings.

Those No-Doubt-About-It Infidelity Blues

Like a throw of shot silk,
its blue brilliance
calmed by the iron,
completed,
so you can clearly see
the alternative versions.

This is the first thing,
The first thing you feel
When you happen to find
That the worst thing,
The worst thing that could happen,
Has happened for real.

And everything adds up to a pattern,
So that it's certain now,
As if there's somehow a curtain
Drawn back in your mind.

Like someone blind
seeing the sunlight, dazed
by daylight and all the colours
hidden in water
transparent out of the tap,
invisible to ordinary seers.

That time my pa shaved off his beard
The man we knew just disappeared,
Unrecognizably himself,
Which was truly false and falsely weird.

Like understanding all 'fortie partes',
all eight choirs, of *Spem in alium*,
a mirage of 'Mr Tallys',
wave after overlapping wave,
understanding at last the palimpsest sea,
even down to the discords.

This is the first thing,
The first thing you feel
When you happen to find
That the worst thing,
The worst thing that could happen,
Has happened for real.

And everything adds up to a pattern,
So that it's certain now,
As if there's somehow a curtain
Drawn back in your mind.

Like the Arrivals and Departures board:
that sudden solitaire sequence,
that drop-down cascade,
revolving itself, resolving itself,
arriving at certainty,
at bottom.

That time my pa shaved off his beard
The man we knew just disappeared,
Unrecognizably himself,
Which was truly false and falsely weird.

Like a tense tangle of twine
suddenly simplified, submissive
to the perfect pull,
fluent, flowing, continuous,
leading you straight to the heart
of your labyrinth.

This is the first thing,
The first thing you feel
When you happen to find
That the worst thing,
The worst thing that could happen,
Has happened for real.

And everything adds up to a pattern,
So that it's certain now,
As if there's somehow a curtain
Drawn back in your mind.

Like a woman reaching her climax
after an incoherent journey
through unreliable, dirty terrain:
that clench of recognition
and the tingle of the aftershock.
Every detour was leading to this.

That time my pa shaved off his beard
The man we knew just disappeared,
Unrecognizably himself,
Which was truly false and falsely weird.

This is the first thing,
The first thing you feel
When you happen to find
That the worst thing,
The worst thing that could happen,
Has happened for real
And everything adds up to a pattern,
So that it's certain now,
As if there's somehow a curtain
Drawn back in your mind.

Like falling in love
at first sight, first sight
invested with second sight,
our irresistible, inevitable,
elective affinity,
the perfect chemistry of us.

Davos Documentary B&W

Chalets packed in Styrofoam.
A black and white world,
winter's approximate documentary.

Ski lifts tireless as a trail of ants.
Then stopped,
a charm bracelet.

A single snowflake
touches my lip, tingles
like a cold sore.

Convulsed with calling, calling –
so the sound can be seen –
this magpie in the firs.

It drops, unstoppably straight,
for fifteen feet,
then lands,
with a gulp,
on a lower branch.

The swallow dive.
Its meaning divined.
Nothing to do with the bird.
All to do with the gullet.

The firs are herring-bone with snow.
A fur coat of pelts,
keeping the mountain cold.

Groomers prowl the pistes at night,
Blake's unsleeping tyger,
dangerous in the darkness.

And the stars so near.
The evening star
big as an aircraft
close to emergency landing...

We ski in our sleep,
schuss in the brace position.
Foetal, flying, fast-forward film.

L. F. Rosen: Three Poems

GENETICS

A cold winter night.
You might have hit your head
the stars are so painfully close.

Life is like an ampoule in your pockets
where your two clenched hands
are cupping the fire of all creation –
the smoor of smouldering moorland.

Your hands where your lifeline joins
your father's father's father's father's –
every one of them
and every one of their wives.

This endless epic
in two hidden hands.

Take them out of your pockets.

Show them to the cold winter night.
Read the route map written there.
Lines meet. Lives meet. Ancestry
in the imprint of a fingernail.
Man meets child.
Each hand a bookmark
of before and after.
For as long as you live.

THAT'S HOW IT WILL BE

You stand in the door.
You wait. You call them in
to the faint friction of clean cotton sheets
covering the cots in the attic.

And all you can see coming closer
is a dog. The rise and fall of his shoulder blades.
Steam like lint along the length of his back.
The catarrh of his growl. His paws on the path.

And suddenly his muzzle fits to your hands,
but the head winces away, tosses to rid itself
of something sticky, something stale, something sour,
something that could be loneliness.

THE STORY OF FIRE

I was a wolf
so my nose gave some thought to the smell.
The smell remembered another smell –
the headlong ache of urine
left by animals in flight.

Closer to, I could make out
the strips they fed to the fire –
a black rash of bubbles
on a small squirming fire.

I knew fire. But this was different.
It was pink. Like a newborn.
And cared for by the pack of ragged animals –
with their backs to the night,
as if fire could confer
a childish kind of confidence.

But however hard they fed it with scraps,
the fire seemed determined to die.
With its last throes,
it licked their hands, it licked their faces,
looking for love.

Then one of the animals stood,
and the fur fell to his feet. With a stick,
he began to beat the fire.
All hell broke loose, great ragged tongues
ransacking the heavens for food.

I was curious. I came closer.
Then the hotness banged shut in my face.
That was when I learned that fire is a door.
I stopped. But I could not stop myself
sampling the scorched smell of skin
on that hairless back.

It bared its teeth. It threw me a bone.
I found its eye and found my body
flattened to the earth, afraid.
That night, I slept by the fire,
dreaming the old dreams,
troubled with new dreams.

Marcel's Fancy-Dress Party

For Jan Eijkelboom, poet and translator
On his eightieth birthday
1 March 2006

Au premier moment je ne compris pas pourquoi j'hésitais à
reconnaître le maître de maison, les invités, et pourquoi
chacun semblait s'être 'fait une tête', générallement poudrée
et qui les changeait complètement.

– Proust, *Le temps retrouvé*

When we floss our teeth
we look like Francis Bacon's
screaming Popes.

How does it feel, Jan,
to be translated –
so quickly, so brilliantly,

so unfaithfully,
into old age?
Into this convincing,

irresistibly plausible
eighty-year-old
everyone is persuaded by?

That seems to everyone original.
Not a version, not an imitation,
not approximate at all.

Only two minutes ago,
you were so young and biological
you were hardly you.

You were biology itself.
Even now you are exactly the same,
you feel exactly the same,

but you are different.
Your body speaks another language
you don't quite understand.

You have the rudiments.
But it isn't fluent.
You wonder,

is it possible to flirt
in this foreign language?
Is it possible to write

another kind of love poetry,
awkward in your mouth,
where you might welcome want?

And you wait, patiently,
still with your full head of hair,
for the electric toothbrush

to reach its reliable shudder
of happiness – infallible
in your fallible hand.

High Table

The Senior Fellow's semi-shaven Adam's apple
shifty on the frayed collar of his check shirt.

Massaging gold,
thumb and index finger
soothe his signet ring.
An osculation. A frig. On his little finger.

Impatient. He pushes back his cuff,
consults the scratched three-quarter face.
And catches the Butler's professionally placid eye.
'We can't wait any longer for the chaplain.'

The chaplain is on her knees,

her trousered knees, gowned, dog-collared,
pushing a prepuce back, down,
with finger and thumb.

If you look,
you can just make out
the label (Russell and Bromley)
pricing her pair of black Oxfords.
There. See. At the pale pristine instep.

Anointing the glans
with its glycerine.

A hand on her head,
blessing and forcing.

Catching the chrism on her tongue.
Two small drops. Quick. Not copious.

On her feet.

And running.
Now diagonally across the quad,
caught in the commotion of her gown,
plucked, enveloped, billowing black.

The inescapable smoke of her gown,
streaming, rips and tears at the sleeves.
Running.
The smack of her shoes on the wet flags
rhyming in the cloisters.
A squash court of echoes,
intense rally of echoes.

Taking the steps to Hall
two at a time.

Steady. Still her breathing. Stroll.
Pull the points of her waistcoat down.

The gavel is poised. Brought down.
The Butler draws back the chair
at the head of High Table.
The Senior Fellow rises. The Fellows follow, stand.
A long Latin grace
leaves the lips of the senior scholar
gracelessly, a gabble of echoes.

See the seams of the servants' skirts,
the trouser seams, and the thumbs
at attention along the line of each seam.

The chaplain freeze-framed
in the body of the Hall.
Her dog collar's dim smile,
grey-white sperm.

Candle flames curtsy and stretch.
Relax and flex. Flex and relax.

Amen.

————

Exterior. Traffic lights. Daytime.
The next day.

Peterhouse reflected, curved
across a crash helmet's black visor.

Gauntlets gripping
the high handlebars of a chopped hog.

The right hand
flexing, relaxing,
retaining the revs,
the engine's excitement,

then roaring away
with open throttle
down Trumpington Street
as the traffic lights change.

———————

Heaving the Harley-Davidson
onto its stand. Resistance, weight. Flex
and relax.

Planted. In the kitchen quad.
Bling of chrome. The tyre treads
plaited like corn rows.

Gauntlets tight under his armpit.
Fingers fidget with the helmet fastening.

Towards you, towards you,
folds of leather
relax and flex
as the crotch comes into close-up.

———————

Serried on the tabletop,
dull with Goddard's Silver Dip,
brightness breathed on, slandered,
clouded, smeared, opaque,
silver salvers, silver sugar dredgers,
candelabras, candlesticks, teapots.

Each item
stagnant as a stage-mirror.

Silver cutlery is kept sheathed
in pocketed baize scrolls
which tie with tabs.
Twelve items per scroll.
They open out like cloth toolkits.

Thrown on the table like a trophy,
the black helmet,
then the gauntlets' challenge.

Gauntleted herself in pink rubber gloves,
Angelika hardly looks up
from the fork she is frigging clean.

Then she slowly caresses
the curve of a candelabra,
the rise of a spout.
With gangrened fingertips.

Nylon z-zzzzz-zzzzzip unzipped
like a Yamaha
flicking through corners,
going through gears.
He sheds his leathers,
naked under them.

For a moment, he is Marsyas,
upper body hanging, peeled
to the pubic bone.

Scrotum sways as he shrugs out of his leathers,
shaking a leg,
shaking the other leg free.

Stands in the kitchen dusk,
clean as a candle,
whiter than wax,
a source of light.

There are two things to notice:
the scooped curves
where his buttocks tense,
the different, tightening browns
of his furrow, foreskin and balls.

Then he becomes the Butler.

Coaxing cufflinks into the crack
of each starched cuff, yes,
cramming buttons through crevices.
Glances into the mirror,
and folds down his collar,
trapping his black tie.
Adjusts the silk: a slither
of changing length and width
alive in the fold of his collar.

Wrapping the slick round the slack,
feeding silk into itself.
Tightening. Tightening.
Working the solid knot
into the V.

Then the throb of buttons
along the length of his brocaded waistcoat,
mother-of-pearl
quick under his fingers,
one after one after one…

He studies his face in the mirror.
Neutral. Fair-haired. Forty.
Smoothing his eyebrows with spit.

Angelika still at the kitchen table,
masturbating a tablespoon,
mechanically, getting a glitter.

They haven't exchanged a word.

———————

In Hall, the servants are laying High Table.
On a simple piece of polished wood,
napkins like amulets, tumblers,
two wine glasses per place.

Cold, clear jugs of cubist water,
iced with angles and semi-opaque planes.

The pattern of cutlery,
orderly as surgical instruments,
or a percussionist's frieze.
Or the repeat in a Mexican blanket.

An elaborately chased silver-gilt
seventeenth-century kissing cup
will captivate the quarter-tones
of candlelight.

―――――

Interior. The Butler's pantry.
He angles the corkscrew
and insinuates its length

(mice-squeaks
mute to obscene murmur)

deep in the Cantenac-Brown,
a decent Margaux for a Guest Night.
Better than decent. Almost indecent.
3ième cru classé, 1994. Perfect for drinking.

The cork resists, then
comes, with a little gasp.

He passes the drawn cork,
dark as a Tampax, under his nostrils.

Winds out the corkscrew,
begins on the next. Scoring
the soft heavy foil,
winding it off.

The camp, pantomime smooch
of further corks coming out.

———————

Angelika leans to her left,
to balance the weight of the wines
in the crook of her arm.
Four bottles to each wicker basket.

At the base of her biceps
(bulging, the size of a Kiwi fruit)
two visible tendons.

On her tiny hard muscle,
a definite grey-blue vein,
slightly twisted.

A kink in the vein
that fascinates the eye.

But we are behind her behind,
its altering outline in her tight black trousers.

Its fluent flesh,
repeating a ritual.

Continuity. Change.
Weight. Counter-weight.
Simple scales.
The slow tip, the languid rise.

Simple scales
in slow motion.
Practising perfection.
Left hand. Then right hand.
Now both hands together.

Mechanics as music.
Its mystery obvious
and impossible to analyse.

See its rise and fall,
flex and relax,
and fail to finish your sentence

for the singing, the singing,
melody flooding your mind.

Angelika can interrupt
the Regius Professor of Divinity
talking to the Regius Professor of Ecclesiastical History.

———————

Thursday. Guest Night.

Neither Regius Professor is dining tonight.

The college fields
its President, the President's wife,

two bachelor heterosexual dons,
Bennett, Computing Science,
Ainsworth, English (Early Modern);

the Newton Professor of Physics.
(Rasmus Petersen, her guest, has won a Nobel Prize,
for work on genetics.)

Alan Howard, the Music Fellow,
a cripple, whose guest
(there are only two guests)
is the writer Ralph Clifford.

Finally, Farley, the Russian don.

Nine. A modest midweek total.

(One of the waiters,
out of Wisconsin, out of funds,
is doing his doctorate on Wittgenstein.)

————

Sir Alan, the President,
is already fortified
before he lifts to the light
(two streamers of bubbles,
twin towers of tiny fish eggs
perfectly balanced)
his second glass of champagne:
'Wonderful stuff, alcohol.
Over-the-counter sodium pentothal.
I used to be a chemist,'
he explains to Clifford in the Common Room.
'Tell me you used to be a writer.'

'I write fiction. Novels. Short stories.'
Clifford is famous, internationally known.
Famous enough to ignore
the President's feigned ignorance.
Also forewarned. He knows what to expect.

'Not recently, I hear.
I hear you're blocked.'
Booze: the President's problem
takes the form of 'candour'.
(Call it deliberate rudeness.)

Otherwise the problem is invisible.

Howard, the crippled Music Fellow,
looks much drunker than the President:
toppling on his two sticks
coming across the rucked kilim
to rescue his guest.

(There used to be a wooden toy,
a leggy foal, say, or a calf,
with limbs in elasticated sections:
alert, erect, poised on a plinth,
it detumesced
when you pressed a spring.
Then sprang up again.
Howard is poised when parked
– those steepled, attentive hands –
dishevelled, disintegrating when he walks.
'Left in the lurch.' Howard's joke.)

————

Ainsworth (English, Early Modern)
sports a single silver earring
through a fleshy lobe,
shirt-tail outside his trousers,
a casual, meticulously maintained,
two-day growth of beard,
rings on his thumbs:
a self-conscious semiology

that signals
one unpedantic pedagogue,
unpredictable, exciting, *young*.

He is 30 and explaining,
not for the first time,
the etymology of 'insincere'.

Apparently, the Latin for 'wax' is *cera*
and the Latin for 'without' is *sine*.
'When the Romans bought a marble sculpture,
you see, the flaws were concealed with wax.
So a flawless piece of marble
was "sincere", without wax.'

The President contemplates his wine
and interrupts:
'Dr Ainsworth, spare us your party piece.
You're like a character in Chekhov.
A minor character. A schoolmaster
restricted to one rigmarole.
Whose wife is being swived
by the local landowner.
The only alternative to etymology.
Bloody good Margaux.'

Ainsworth irrepressible, erroneous:
'The etymology of "swived"
is from the Anglo-Saxon *swinken*.
Which means to work.
Swinken is a strong verb, so…'

The President:
'A minor character,
but a major irritation.'

Ainsworth confides to Clifford:
'We endure the President's impatience
patiently. Sometimes High Table
resembles Out Patients at the Fulbourn.'

Ainsworth pleased with his playful syllables.
He will repeat them.
Like a minor character in Chekhov.

'The Fulbourn is a mental hospital.'
Footnote for the benefit of Clifford.

———————

Rasmus Petersen is bald.
Freckled as a curlew's egg.
Nearly 70 now, he refuses to believe
his best work behind him:
'Once we isolate those genes
that cause the undesirable effects…'

The Newton Professor of Physics,
his host, Pamela Johansson,
interrupts –

an exasperated lesbian,
she has heard it before

– confides to Petersen
that Angelika (or Angelika's arse)
should have an honorary fellowship
for sterling service to the college.

Nods in its direction.

Its gravitas,
its wag.

The Nobel Laureate,
stopped in his tract.

————

Lady Charlotte, Charlie Rowth,
the President's wife,
with tumbleweed hair
and misbuttoned blouse
(the dangling brooch, upside down,
Charlie's concession to evening wear)
extends her filthy fingernails
to say:

'If it wasn't for *these,*'

(across her chest,
her gardening hands,
like gardening gloves,
clutch, but fail to cover,
her extensive breasts)

'I'd be a tighthead prop.
Or a lock forward.
If it wasn't for these.'

Pamela Johansson speaks across High Table:
'Charlie, you do know, don't you,
that a women's rugger team exists?'

———————

Interior. SCR lavatories.

Mahogany seats. Splash back.
The urinal flushes:
an awkward, injured fan,
as if someone had opened
a shaken soda water.
Farley, the Fellow in Russian,
is showing his breasts to Bennett,
Computing don.

Explaining the areolas.
'The miracle of oestrogen.
You want them to be right.'

He cups the little tits
in his hands. Looks in the mirror.

Bennett thinks:
But your hands will always be male.

He says:
'Angelika better look to her laurels.'

And Farley:
'Still harping on his daughter.'

———————

Interior. Candlelight. Common Room.
Silver liquid in light.
Small laboratory of wines:
more Margaux, port, sauterne, an Alsace Riesling.
A shingle beach of nuts.
The fools' gold of Ferrero Rocher.
That ole Black Magic.
A ruined ziggurat of cherries.

Ainsworth is explaining
innuendo in Laurence Sterne.

Turning up the volume of his ring,
he lectures his glass of Fonseca '65:
'Behind the simpering pretence
of sensibility, Larry the Lad –

deliberate dirty-mindedness.
(I quote the other Lawrence,
D. H., David Herbert, Bertie Lawrence,
on Jimmy Joyce's *Ulysses*).'

The President to Ralph Clifford,
an audible aside:
'Dr Ainsworth is on first-name terms
with every author on the syllabus.
As we address the college servants.
Claret helps.'

Ainsworth, unabashed, uninterrupted:
'Deliberate dirty-mindedness
which defies our censure.
Why? Because we are complicit.
All innuendo requires autocomplete.
Which shows we're made of Sterner stuff.'

The President's migraine voice:
'Something he prepared earlier.'

'In *A Sentimental Journey*,
he was the Graham Norton of his day,
comedian also Queer Theorist.
"The Theorist as Artist":
(I adapt from Oscar the intersexualist.)
Nothing he could not sexualize:
quills and inkwells, thimbles, gloves,
gloves, my God, the neck of a purse,
threading a needle. The old in-out.'

The President confides to the tablecloth:
'Ainsworth, you could blight Angelika's arse.'

In fact, Ainsworth has it in mind –
Angelika's arse.

———————

Rasmus on his hobby-horse:
'So, via genetics, the genius of Mozart.'
He wards off interruption
with a palsied hand.

But Alan Howard intervenes:
'Yes, the genius of Mozart.
True, he transcribed Allegri's *Miserere*
after hearing it once in the Sistine Chapel.
Once, and once only. Aged 14.
A famous feat of musical memory.
Generally designated "genius".'
Howard lifts his own pale hand.

And pushes away the pale china plate
with his other fine fingers.
On it two tiny planets –
his still life of cherry stones.

'But, Rasmus, the autograph of K. 385
records a clutch of second-thoughts,
of hesitations, alternatives.
He composed, corrected, made mistakes,
Corrected. Thought twice, improved.
We can see him thinking the music through.
It wasn't dictation from the deity.'

Mozart's tendency to 'take dictation':
light-fingered virtuoso at the keyboard...
Howard's head,
the head of a Hollywood star,
remembers (but keeps in reserve)
Muzio Clementi and *Die Zauberflöte*.

Rasmus responds:
'Exactly. Exactly. I agree. Exactly *that*.
By engineering to *improve* the DNA.
To correct the chromosome
and eliminate mistakes.
We screen for abnormalities.
The gene for, for example, homosexuality.'

'What about screening for baldness?'
Pamela Johansson *lesbian ad hominem*.
'That's pretty undesirable.'

And Howard:
'I accept I differ from the norm.
Impossible with spina bifida
to walk with ease.
Lumbar procedures
keep hydrocephalus at bay.
This isn't merely tiresome.'

He falters.
Wondering whether to risk
his reputation for wry urbanity.

'I am too ashamed
to take my clothes off…
even for a prostitute.'

Sex. Two cherry stones.
The meagreness.

And a line of George Herbert
like heartache in his head:
'Love bade me welcome…'

Love. The heart in free fall,
giving up the ghost to gravity,
safe in someone's arms.

Close to tears
which he keeps from his voice:
'But I wouldn't want
to be weeded out. By anyone.'

———————

Interior. The Butler's pantry.
Angelika leans her hands and arse
along the edge of his desk.

Talking down
to the Butler sprawled in his chair.
Tie an off-duty, off-centre Y.

She says:
'He's a fantastic writer.
I've read everything he's written.
My Auntie Mary, *The Love Bird*,
A Table for Three. *Chinese Chopsticks*
is one of my favourite books.
I have to speak to him.
Taiga's a set-text.'

The Butler,
licking the length of a roll-up:
'Go ahead. Feel free.
But I wouldn't if I were you.
It's not the servant thing – '
Zippo poised,
then lit with practised expertise –
a Karate move. Chop-chop.
And as swiftly extinguished.
'College is too full of cant
to put you in your place.
I just don't like the look of him.
He's got those actor's eyes –
always making eye contact.
You only fill his fucking glass
and you get the comether.'

Angelika:
'You're jealous.
It's just my beautiful backside.'

The Butler:
'Listen. *I* pour the wine. Not you.
Man or woman. Makes no difference.'
He stares, unseeing, at the desk. Remembering.
Depth of focus. Quiet intensity. *Italics.*
'Something extra in the way they look.
Hitler had it. Clinton. Blair. You feel *seen.*
And it's automatic. Pure technique.
You know when someone gives your hand a squeeze?
They do it, only with their eyes.
And it's only the eyes.'

Angelika:
'He's a great writer.'

The Butler,
forking his hair with his fingers,
yawning like a tragic mask:
'Suit yourself.
You always do.'

And she:
'I get it from you.'

Then he:
'Well, you don't take after her.
Not that I can see.'

He thinks of asking
about his bitter better half –
then thinks better of it.

————

Interior. Common Room.
Incontinent candles
squat in grease.
Ralph Clifford is telling Angelika
all about art. All about art:
that narrative, the best narrative,
flirts with the reader.
A flirtation that is sometimes a cock-tease.
Sometimes a tremendous fuck.

(He has drunk quite a lot.)

(Ainsworth, seeing himself outbid,
is silenced, sits with his eyes shut.
Injections of heartburn.)

'Life is trivial. Death is trivial.
None of this matters. Obviously.
Art is our pretence
that people are important.
It is our consolation.
Yes? Do you read me?'

Howard, Sir Alan, Charlie, Rasmus Petersen,
Ainsworth, Farley, Bennett, Pamela Johansson,
listen, unimportant, to his aria.

She can read him.

Attentive, shrewd Angelika
meditates on what the Butler saw:
her eyed-up arse,
that automatic charm,
the reflex hints
of the habitually sexual,
his actual indifference.

'Once, religion soothed
our sense of insignificance.
The fall of a sparrow.
Nothing too negligible.
Lear expresses the opposite –
outrage at our unimportance.
"Why should a dog, a horse, a rat, have life,
And thou no breath at all?"
Our fucked-off friends may feel exploited
when they find they're in our books,
but what will survive of us,
and them, is art.'

Angelika the extra-muralist,
part time at the CFE,
interrupts and amplifies:
'Like that Stoppard play,
when the playwright character
Harry says (*The Real Thing*,
just after the cricket bat bit)
that if you get the words right,
children will speak your poem for you
even though you're dead and gone.'

Awkward with high seriousness.
She has lost her reservations,
about herself, about Ralph Clifford,
faltered into confidence.
Ready to hit the high notes
in a well-read duet.
Her body a sound board:
one thickness spruce, special taper, sugar pine ribs…

Jealous Ainsworth, across the Common Room,
without opening his eyes:
'Then his wife, the actress, Annie,
recites what's written in his typewriter:
79. Interior. Commander's capsule.
He's working on a Sci-Fi film script.
Tommy Straussler, aka Stoppard,
downsizing the writer's ego.
Thank Christ. Not before time.
And it's Henry. Not Harry.'

Angelika silenced.
Academic Ainsworth cannot resist.
Even if, so up his own arse,
the know-all knows
he's kissing kissing Angelika's arse
goodbye for good.

The President addresses the ceiling:
'Dr Ainsworth's bedside manner,
my dear. His way of wooing.'

And to Ainsworth:
'Why not simply ask the girl
to clear up, then clear out?'

And to Ralph Clifford:
'Ego sufficiently downsized?'

How to make an embryonic situation
explicit and impossible: thinks Howard.
Tactlessly rebuking the tactless.

Silence.

Sitting for a group portrait. So still.

More silence.

The President begins
to blow the candles out.
Small rococo smoke.
The acrid stink of ear-wax.

———————

Bennett (Computer Sciences),
nude, up in the Old Tower,
is on his bare knees,
caressing his father's Mannlicher,
Angelika caught in the night sights.
She and the Butler
in aquarium light
laid back on the Harley-Davidson,
as it weaves, waddles,
to the college main gate.
Like Groucho Marx
he walks his Harley-Davidson.
As if it were a hobby-horse.

Bennett has asked her out. Twice.
And been refused, politely.
'My father forbids fraternisation
between staff and the SCR.'

(*Still harping on the daughter.*)

Bennett: of no importance.
And difficult to describe.
Nondescript nonentity. Dry skin.
Brittle, dusty hair,
strimmed rather than cut.
Brilliant, border-autistic,
when he talks
his head infinitesimally moves,
in synch to his lips.

Obsessed by Angelika.

Like everyone else.

When he comes,
in his head
he is holding her down.

Invisible.

Visible.

For Pat Kavanagh

dark steps
across this pale grass
perfect with dew,

dark steps
so early, so swift,
the short length of this long lawn…

On the Slopes

Because the bubble down was broken,
we took the chair instead, went up
and skied back down – to the black,
the black we knew was closed:
'risk of avalanche'.

We weren't afraid: my son and I
had skied the black already. Twice that week.
It was bald in places. Soil and stone.
Tricky, not dangerous. No signs of avalanche.

We reassured my daughter.
The piste was now unmarked
(fasces, bundles by the edges),
but we knew the way it went.

I fell, for the first time,
negotiating moguls,
neither steep, nor difficult –

except that snow had fallen overnight
and then the sun had shone all day
so the moguls were heavy. Sluggish.
A wet weighty eiderdown.
The mood of the snow had changed
to moodiness.

The slope seemed readable enough,
but the punctuation was unpredictable.

It was like ironing starch.
Sticky. Awkward. Slow and sudden.

Then my son fell. With a laugh.
We continued, skiing carefully.

The second time I fell,
as I up-ended, both skis came off.

One ski silently, slowly at first,
slid away down the hill, for twenty yards.
I watched it like a whisper.

Inaudible. Unreachable.
An anchorite serene beyond desire.
A long ship anchored in listless surf.

The other ski behaved itself,
its brakes snagged in the snow –
those wire-traps on the bindings,
paraplegic, trailing like heron legs.

My daughter and my son looked down
from the top of the gulley opposite.
Throwing the useless ski ahead,
I crawled, first down, then up,
towards them. A matter of yards.

It was easier to roll downhill.
That way I didn't sink. My weight was spread.

Crawling up, I became exhausted quickly.
The snow was a swallow reflex.
The surface gave. It wouldn't hold me.
The thirsty turquoise-tinted whiteness would.

Any weight on my arm,
and the arm was in to the armpit.
My leg sank to my crotch.
I had to haul my ski boot out,
only to sink again. And again.

The weight of the ski boot
was trying my weakness.
I weighed its enmity.

My children watched.
They watched and listened.
I was panting. I couldn't speak without a rest.

And then it came to me:
that this is what my dying will be like.

A few feet away, close
yet in another country,
my children simply watching.

Concerned, but unable to help.
Nothing to be done. Or said.

They will listen to amplified breathing,
rasping like a tracheotomy,

as their father tries and tries
for the top of this small hill,
this impossible, trivial distance,
to where his lungs can rest,
to where it will be possible to stop.

Nothing they can do. Nothing they can say.
They only watch.
There will be no rescue.
My children will be patient, patient,
waiting for the last breath quiet as the creak of snow.

A la recherche du temps perdu

like a thing that falls through water, she passes away…

– Oscar Wilde, 'The Critic as Artist'

So I turn to a dead language again:
ineo, I go into, enter, begin.

Doleo, I am in pain, I grieve.
and everyone thinks I am being brave.

Ignis, ignis, masculine, fire:
at St Pancras Crematorium, I stare,

light-headed with caffeine,
at the light-oak coffin,

wondering what I feel, where I stand.
Vulnus, vulneris, neuter, a wound.

I watch the coffin vanish
to Mozart on tape, its varnish

about to come up in blisters
and burst into a boa

of full-length, rustling fire,
just as we reach the *Dies Irae*.

Sinews shrink from the flames.
Sinews shrink in the flames.

I sentimentalize
and then revise.

Iter, itineris, neuter, a journey.
Without end. Where the road is empty.

Sine plus ablative, without.
The words are in my mouth

but I can't teach myself
the simple, difficult lesson of grief.

Too terrible to learn. Too hard
to have the words by heart.

I can't accept you're dead.
You're still here, in my head:

irritating, prickly, unsalved,
unsolved, unlovable, loved.

That bubble at the corner of your mouth.
Which seems somehow to mean so much.

————

Sometimes unlovable.
Not always. And always beautiful.

Except for your beard,
which you hated, and I adored.

Which neither of us spoke about.
I was kept quiet

by your behaviour.
You behaved as if it wasn't there.

Whereas it was, one of the facts,
like the long guard hairs on a fox.

Twenty. Just under the chin. Peroxide
let them flourish in disguise.

Or you clipped them with fine scissors,
made in Germany, curvilinear,

kept at the back of a drawer –
hidden, but not hidden, like the hairs.

Almost oriental when they grew back:
tiny, shining, sparse, glint-black

like surgical stitches.
Tweezers raised unsightly blotches.

A student I taught Wyatt and Surrey
dropped his tweezers in my study,

a flinch of light in the carpet pile.
His nose was heartily male.

'They fle from me that sometyme did me tweke.'
Hypocrite, you laughed at my joke:

we never talked about any of this
until, after we split, electrolysis

also took permanent care
of all nine of your nipple hairs.

We were in bed together,
talking like sister and brother.

For once. Your black boyfriend
objected to them, so that was the end.

I said, the guy's got to be mad.
Those things were a turn-on, I said.

And they were.
Your long glowing nipples shabby with hairs.

Big tits, you laughed. *Men love melons.
Size. They might as well be melons,*

*for all the pleasure I feel.
They do nothing for me at all.*

What has all this to do with anyone else?
Why all these intimate details?

You introduced me to Conrad's fiction.
The Nigger and its introduction,

which says the writer makes things real.
His task: 'to make you hear, to make you feel –

It is, before all, to make you *see*.'
To make you *see*. Before all. I agree.

'That – and no more, and it is everything.'
Details that make you cringe

will make the reader *see*,
see the self you showed to me.

The vulgar fraction and the better half.
Shaving your legs in the bath

like Rembrandt in a shower cap.
The razor's satin stripe through soap

like sap. Your shaven legs
sleek and sexual as stripped twigs.

You putting in a contact lens,
taking a new moon out of the cleanser,

meniscus at your fingertip.
You prise open the eyelid

and bend your head,
touch the eye as if it were hot,

a single dab, once,
like a wince

away from something dark,
shielding your face from shock.

Like someone warding off fate,
just a second too late.

Blink-blinking away the tears,
you could *see*. Were one of the seers.

(Turning aside
from AIDS…)

———————

Tea. In your kitchen at Gillespie Road.
We talked about AIDS,

just after the genital herpes scare.
What, 1982, '83? There or round about there.

You were stanching a cold with a Kleenex
you plucked from its box

like a conjuror.
It became damper and smaller,

barely visible up your sleeve.
The size of a semibreve.

You almost made it disappear.
But not quite. It was still there.

Light-hearted, fatalistic,
you made light of it:

Well, you grinned, *I've fucked everyone.*
And you sipped your lapsang souchong.

(The odd white prole,
but black boys on the whole.

For preference a pick-up on the Tube.
Tea the invariable prelude –

to calm their nerves – and talk.
Talk till they could believe their luck.)

Glenn Gould, then, singing along
to the 'Goldberg' Variations

in the sitting room, up the stairs
pairs and pairs and pairs

of handworked, high-heeled cowboy boots
(none, you said, the ideal style or fit)

and the photograph of you nude,
silver gelatin mounted on rag board,

on the bedroom wall,
showing nothing at all.

Nothing at all because
you are hugging your knees,

teeth wet, mouth wide,
thrown back hair and head.

Not quite *Vogue*, but beautiful.
You wanted to model

after you chucked your lecturing job.
You thought you'd give it a stab

and get together a photo-file.
You hired a professional

who fucked you on the studio bed
after he'd taken his shots of you naked.

In fact,
it wasn't a fuck.

It was a quick
suck.

Thirty seconds max.
He was really after a sandwich

with you and his girlfriend.
Which wasn't what you had in mind.

What happened, happened.
Were you innocent?

Surprised by all that juice and joy?
Or on the lookout for a guy

where context might speed things up?
Snow White? Or Snow White drinking 7 Up?

It was your first adventure
with a total stranger.

And that was your modelling career.
Nothing else came of the idea,

except one solitary job for the *BMJ*:
Cystitis: Before and After. Relief Today.

All this, all this is why
no one saw me cry

the morning of your funeral.
My head was full

of grief and dates and calculations.
You'd chosen quotations

from Holub and Ruskin
but I could hardly listen.

I was trying to decide
whether you could have given me AIDS.

And my mind was busy,
watching you write an essay,

stretched out on the floor,
right hand holding your Sheaffer,

left hand propping your chin
just off the floor of the coffin,

lips pulled apart at the corner,
inside out, a urethra,

disclosing a seed of saliva
like dull Russian silver.

————

Miss Mary Lascelles at Somerville,
giving you a tutorial –

May we lay your written work
on the hearth-rug, so to speak?

Strangely appropriate,
since that's where you always scribbled it.

————

In my study,
Torso of a Young Woman by Brancusi,

open on the book rest,
virginal, undressed, a paradox,

and behind,
tied with tartan twine,

a year of your letters from Strasbourg.
Chaste. Factual. An epistolary iceberg.

Trace-elements of you everywhere:
I used to own your *Petit Robert*,

your boxed set of *La Traviata*,
a reproduction of August Macke –

all spoils of the break
until you claimed them back.

And I still possess
a grey chiffon dress

like a wisp of smoke,
clinging, weak,

a wardrobe stranger
on its stolen Harrods hanger.

You taught me your taste
as if I had to pass a test.

I'd adopted student standards:
bookshelves of bricks and chipboard,

the copper alarm clock
with the ping-pong tick,

ten Picasso bullfight posters,
Nescafé, Morphy Richards toaster

with emerald fern design,
one piece of stripped pine…

I was a kind of Deist with a small *d*:
whatever was, was OK by me,

even the landlord's floral curtains.
You, though, were scathing and certain:

you had visiting cards
(which you ironized: 'I deferred

to my father's anachronistic notion
of student customs…'),

cut glass, a cafetière,
Mexican rugs, Struwwelpeter hair,

ballet pumps with gathered soles.
You were bilingual,

had been taught Sidney (not Wyatt)
by 'the writer, Antonia Byatt',

and at a fire-balloon party
given by Francis Huxley,

the nephew of Aldous,
you spilled a dish of peanuts

on his parquet floor.
Beautiful. Just leave them there,

he said, and you were impressed.
I was jealous, depressed

and faintly rebellious for once.
I wouldn't concede an inch.

I'd stub a fag out on the floor
and say: *Beautiful. Just leave it there.*

It really pissed you off. Thirty years on,
I think I'm my own man

but I have two 8-day clocks
with barely audible ticks,

and *figures* round the face,
not Roman numerals or milled spaces,

a Swiza and an Angelus,
as if you'd made the purchase.

You also formed my sexual tastes
by certain physical traits –

the way your knees whispered together
like words of a feather –

by alterations to my 'technique'
so that it suited yourself.

You taught me sex
was conversation and not a speech.

I wrote poetry to impress you
and you're in my writing, too:

if a woman scratches her face
that's you leaving your trace,

or counts the hairs in her brush,
or parts the hair of her bush…

You're everywhere. So it isn't odd
if there are traces of you in my blood…

———

Listening to 'A Whiter Shade of Pale',
galley slaves of the bar football.

———

Tunis. The palm trees' structure
is file and feather duster.

The sea is sparking like sandpaper.
Arabic script, its ripple and flutter

stencilled on whitewash.
The main café: a line of hookahs

like a single letter
practising itself. On the river,

a Muslim oarsman rowing to Mecca.
You are in school. Your teacher

points to your grave 9-year-old face:
la seule étoile de la classe.

One boy ironically claps.
Wind works through the palm tops.

The edge of a tent
is waving to attract attention.

You showed me your passport once,
a schoolgirl facing the lens,

la seule étoile de la classe
who couldn't settle for less,

whose mouth is already sad.
You never forgot the accolade,

which turned into a reproach
as you waited for the approach

of distinction. Or failure
like Perkin Warbeck or Anastasia.

You'd write. You'd explore the Amazon.
Your father was the bastard son

of Battistini, the Italian baritone or bass.
At Cambridge, he brought *Ulysses*

back from Paris and earned two lines
in *Speak, Memory* – refined

to a pair of initials, P. M.
Meeting him was like meeting a statesman.

He didn't shake hands.
He was silent. He was grand.

You were the suppliant.
He gave you his pronate left hand.

Tunis. Rome. He'd lived abroad.
He pronounced 'billiards' *biyards*.

He was like de Gaulle
awaiting destiny's call,

when the moment for France was ripe.
He called me 'the gutter-snipe'

(years later: he'd forgotten my name)
and frightened the young Michael Frayn,

who was keen on another daughter.
You took after your father,

but you were a literary snob,
exasperated by the successfully glib,

mainly our mutual friends,
the Martins, Julians and Ians,

whose books would always be shallow
unless they got round to Dante and Plato…

You translated Flaubert for Penguin.
La Tentation de Saint Antoine. Pure protein.

And you published a novel
which was 'ambitious' and unreadable.

Even to me, who thought
I might have a walk-on part.

I just couldn't finish it. I tried
again. And again. I should have lied.

You forgave me. There were precedents,
after all: DuCamp passing sentence

(*Burn it!*) on *La Tentation* in manuscript
and Flaubert surviving the verdict…

(Plus long ago I'd gagged at your drafts
of Flaubert's foie gras text.)

By then, you knew you had AIDS.
Jamie had died in the States,

your ex, the black bisexual.
So, what *I* thought was trivial,

especially three years after publication.
(You'd been in Rome: *found my vocation.*

Guess. A job as a gravedigger.
How did that take so long to figure out?)

And you needed a literary executor.
But I was already spoken for,

a huge estate, so I refused.
The AIDS I guessed

and didn't guess.
Was your request a request?

Or a threat? Or a subtle plea?
I guess I didn't want to see.

———

A year later, we were in Fornello's
in Southampton Row:

I was having the chocolate sponge,
you were having a cold revenge.

1990: the last time I saw you.
A tin sun out in the blue.

I gave you my new book of essays
and asked you what you thought of my play.

Of '*1953*'? You shook your head a bit.
I think Racine a very, very, very great poet.

Over the starter of house ravioli,
we'd quarrelled over Misha Maisky.

It was Beethoven with Argerich.
I had a spare ticket

so you came along.
Because Maisky sang along

as he played,
there was a delayed

echo like a transatlantic call,
peripheral, only just audible.

Rueful, you shook your head.
As if the fuss were in my head.

You 'couldn't hear it' until
the very end of the interval,

when we met your pianist friend
who was going before the end

because, because, *because*
of Maisky's horrible humming noise.

Why did I bring it up? No idea.
Shit. Desperate to *praise* your ear,

I remembered from years before
The Vulcan Bulletins by Sam Gulliver.

Sam Gulliver was a pseudonym
for James Hamilton-Patterson.

How could a *poet*?… you said.
And you'd shaken your head.

Title and author:
what an aural obstacle course.

All the cadence
of pick-a-sticks.

He won the Whitbread First Novel Prize,
I said, for something else,

his second novel.
The ethics of that gave you no trouble.

All publishing was corrupt and nasty,
as I should know. I swallowed my pasta.

Outside, you thanked me for lunch,
laughed, and took the plunge.

You were all charm.
You had taken my arm

so it pressed
against your right breast.

Your eyes swam with warmth
as if you loved me more than anything on earth.

Your hair was going grey.
Let's not repeat today.

*Why don't you come
to Gillespie Road sometime?*

An invitation. An invitation
I still can't fathom.

Asexual? A threat? A subtle plea?
Would you have gone to bed with me?

1990. I never saw you again.
You never went up the Amazon.

———

A la recherche du temps perdu.
Your favourite book beside the loo

(actually *Sodome et Gomorrhe*)
in your pied-à-terre

at the top of your parents' house.
Your father pronounced

your reading habits squalid.
Great art had been sullied.

(*Ulysses* must have been unreadable:
Bloom 'calm above his own rising smell'.)

You preferred long books:
you'd read *The Faerie Queene* twice.

Sir Charles Grandison, *Clarissa*,
Tristram Shandy, Chapman's Homer:

You liked them all
but Proust was special.

You never stopped reading Proust.
Marcel in love with someone he disliked.

———

Trinity lawn, effervescent with hailstones,
green eyes, high cheekbones,

wet, your dark brown fine hair
seeded, melting and molecular.

———

Your first poems were brilliant.
Unhappiness fired your talent.

That and the example of Sylvia Plath.
What happened? You doubted their worth.

Became hermetic. Nothing was published
and the impulse fastidiously vanished.

Thirty years later,
there are images I remember:

'a tongue of gravel',
parched, coming out of a cave;

Somerville library, 'old
spines buttered with gold';

sheep's wool snagged on barbed wire
'like the rare, precious hair

of the dead',
written when your father died.

———————

Your first goldfish at Crick Road
vamped in Isadora Duncan mode,

a faintly corpulent Salome,
swathed in chiffon. It was 1970.

Her replacement wore organza,
was slimmer, harder, a fan dancer

in an orange fishtail dress.
Crick Road was a good address

in the right bit of north Oxford,
but you lived in a garden shed,

admittedly with diamond panes.
A dressmaker ran up some curtains.

You raided your father's stores
for porcelain, a 'T'ang' pottery horse,

you had beautiful stones in water
to deepen their colours.

You bought a hideous sofa bed
for us, a double, and hid

its horror under Mexican blankets.
The goldfish were decoration, thankless

inflections of interior design.
But, inside, things were going wrong.

C. S. Lewis's *Allegory of Love*
was somewhere on your shelves,

insisting on space
between the literal surface

and the underlying truth.
Something definitely stank of fish:

the soupçon of bouillabaisse
that last night's intercourse

had left in your cunt.
I wanted sexual excitement.

You wanted a labour of love
where push came to shove

and the clitoris led me a dance.
I felt like a dunce

trying to anticipate
your testy reprimands too late:

too hard, why did you move?
too soft, why don't you move?

What I was doing was quite difficult:
wanking while fucking, braces and belt.

Not from behind. One of your quirks.
But it usually eventually worked.

Your favourite sexual fantasies
were colours and green fields.

It took a week of talk before
you would wear a see-through bra

in bed. A 'scenario' never repeated.
Somehow it felt a bit stilted.

You kept your Pretty Polly hold-ups on
once and I came too soon.

I wanted to experiment.
And if you wouldn't,

I'd find someone who would.
By accident. Not in cold blood.

It wouldn't be my fault.
Then you thought you were going bald.

Counting the hairs. Every morning,
the brush inspection.

In Blackwell's, you saw a new book on Pater
and Arnold, by David Delaura.

You phoned. You'd wept all day.
You came and wept in the V & A –

in case your ideas were in his book.
I advised you to buy, to take a look.

In Strasbourg, the previous year,
I'd startled a rooted fear.

I'd fucked you half dressed,
wearing a leather vest,

and with your knickers on,
cutting into your arsehole and cunt.

At the Musée de l'Œuvre Notre-Dame next day,
we saw Grunëwald's *Les amants trépassés*:

rents in the skin,
blowflies sipping a chancred shin,

riddled with snakes, worm-casts,
earthworms with waterproof elastoplasts,

a toad at her hairless twat.
I wanted the postcard.

You said you felt sick.
Your face was in shock.

When I left, you went through my letters,
burning out filth with your cigarette.

————

Everything goes, everything goes,
except for you cross-legged in bedclothes,

turning to rumple my hair,
then starting to put on your bra

the way that you put on your bra
(circular stitched from British Home Stores)

not both hands blindly behind,
but fastening the catch in front,

turning it round, hauling it up,
and squeezing each arm through its strap.

This simple ceremony lives
for as long as I am alive.

————

In Strasbourg, when I visited you,
you introduced me to *couscous*,

choucroute, priorité à droite.
You were very affectionate.

At the station, you took off my specs
and kissed me all over my face.

I was your 'Wizzledy Man'
and you were pleased to see me again.

We ate a quiche, a quiche Lorraine.
Quiche hadn't reached England then.

I'd borrowed a tent,
though we had to spend

one night in a proper hotel.
So you could dispel

your mother's suspicions.
One night was a sop to your conscience.

With hotels, your mother assumed
it would be separate rooms.

I'd bought a pair of sleeping bags
that zipped together. The latest trick.

Easter. But cold under canvas. It snowed.
The temperature fell below zero.

We listened to the forecast
on your portable before breakfast.

Stuttgart, Frankfurt: *minus zwei.*
München: *minus* fucking *drei.*

Except for us, the little campsite
was completely deserted,

neat and clean with snow.
There was a pale-grey sentry-go

of our footprints
to the camp latrines.

We fucked, then put on our clothes
to sleep in a frozen doze.

We walked to the village and mooned
over the caravan showroom.

In Munich, we saw *Carmen*
and I understood what opera meant

for the very first time.
The singing held me in its arms.

We saw Fellini's *Satyricon*
and *The Reivers* with Steve McQueen.

Halfway through eating *Linzertorte*, say,
in the Residenz café,

or after ten minutes in the Pinakothek,
I'd feel the snow-melt down my neck.

So we bought me a poet's black hat.
I tried a phrase: *das passt mir gut.*

My German was better than yours.
At a distance of thirty years,

we seem close, you and I,
we are almost certainly happy.

Happy without knowing why.
(As, later, unhappy without knowing why.)

Now the reason seems obvious:
we were close because we were close.

We were on top of each other.
The only time we really lived together.

Together and completely on our own.
There were no lodgers, no separate rooms.

My feet must have stunk.
I was using some cortisone junk

for eczema, when what
I had was athlete's foot.

All night in my sleep,
I'd itch my weeping insteps

through my socks.
You were the soul of tact

when I apologized in the morning.
Much better than snoring.

You told me you were awake already
with a sort of nervous malady

which started at boarding school:
except it wasn't your arsehole,

you said you were the same
as Le Pétomane,

and once your cunt started
you couldn't stop farting.

I licked a nostril, kissed your chin.
Never so close again.

An ex-prisoner-of-war
(who pronounced Manchester

as if he were born in Moss Side)
was in charge of the site.

He gave us apples from his store
and, when we left, one apple more

to plant in English ground:
ein Äpfel in der Erde macht viele Bäume.

I visualize the apple now:
white stone broken brown

ulcerated flesh
deliquescent slush

ebony seeds
softening to suede.

———

Early days. I don't remember when.
Caruso singing on Supraphon.

Something light and popular.
'Vieni sul mar'.

A slightly breathless,
deliberate band. (In the brass,

a moustached player
with a naked tuba

on his lap,
giving her a kiss on the lips…)

What's wrong? Why?
I'd seen your heartbroken eyes.

It's nothing, you said.
Just that Caruso died.

———

For breakfast you ate
chocolate fingers, *langues de chat*,

waffles with maple syrup,
Chamonix biscuits, doughnuts,

or Petit Suisse
with sugar. Anything sweet.

———————

Food. At Stoneleigh, Watlington,
one of your lodgers, Michael Western,

was a brilliant cook.
Eels with prunes, chocolate cake,

for 50p each.
A quid for a really memorable lunch,

Like Michael's moussaka
or his pukkha

Elizabeth David coq au vin,
where you paid extra for wine.

You made me give Michael the sack
for blotting his copybook

the first evening he arrived
with a throbbing car on the drive.

He'd thrown his suitcase and holdall
on the landlord's walnut table

and didn't seem to care about the scratch.
Loud music. Louder smell of hash.

When you started to scratch your face,
I agreed to give him notice.

Blood, snot and tears.
Full-blown hysteria.

So he got a month's notice to leave.
And stayed the full month before he moved.

Cooking prawns with wild rice.
Being there. Being nice.

———————

What else do I remember?
Your chrome tea-infuser,

the combination of your cycle lock,
the number of the beast, 6 6 6,

your arsehole's iodines,
hairs like an icon's

calibrated nimbus,
your black smoking bush,

the dark brown lips
labyrinthine as a molten iris.

The most beautiful I've ever seen.
The most beautiful that's ever been.

———————

You pronounced 'barely'
as if it were 'barley'.

I once said to Tim Hilton,
why are you working on Ruskin?

And Tim was furious.
I know the man who made his truss.

I borrowed your teeth for Judina
and gave your cunt to Ivinskaya.

Disjecta membra scattered everywhere,
unrecognisable, through my *œuvre*:

complex, trivial, true.
And now I have re-membered you.

You difficult, lovely, lost masterpiece,
this is my purpose.

To make you real.
To make you see, to make you feel,

to make you hear.

To make you here.

Acknowledgements

Acknowledgements are due to *Areté*, *Talk*, *The Times Literary Supplement*, *Kadmos*, *Turning the Page: Leopard II*, *Poetry Wales*, the *Guardian*, *The Sunday Times*, *Granta*, *Answering Back* (ed. Carol Ann Duffy), *Picador*, the *London Review of Books*, *Tertulian Poems* (ed. Tristan Garel-Jones), *Poetry Review*. 'Rashomon' was commissioned as an opera to open the Zentrum für Kunst and Medientechnologie Karlsruhe in October 1997: the music was written by Alejandro Viñao.

Pawel Pawlikowski suggested High Table as a starting point for a film script – which turned into this poem. Thanks and apologies are due to him. Thanks also to my colleagues Will Poole and Michel Treisman who checked various 'facts'.

The heroine of my poem *A la recherche du temps perdu* died, aged 50, on 16 March 1995. We were lovers from 1967 to 1972, when I ended the relationship. In the academic year 1968–9 she studied at the University of Strasbourg. She was diagnosed HIV-positive in the late 1980s.